Whales

Written by Cindy Barden
Illustrated by Janet Skiles

Whales are mammals,
larger than all others.

Baby whales drink milk from their mothers.

Whales make sounds
as they swim along.

humpback whale

Some whales sing beautiful songs.

A whale is a strong swimmer,
thanks to its tail.

narwhal

See the long horn
on this type of whale.

Some kinds of whales have no teeth.

**Tiny animals called krill
are all they eat.**

Whales with teeth dine

on fish, squid and lobster.

Layers of fat keep whales

beluga whale

warm in cold water.

Whales hold their breath when
they dive under the sea.

bowhead whale

They let out the old air when
they come up to breathe.

Whales are mammals
just like you and me.
They are the largest animals
on land or in the sea.